GO CANOEING!

by
Nicole A. Mansfield

CAPSTONE PRESS
a capstone imprint

Published by Capstone Press, an imprint of Capstone
1710 Roe Crest Drive, North Mankato, Minnesota 56003
capstonepub.com

Library of Congress Cataloging-in-Publication Data
Names: Mansfield, Nicole A., author.
Title: Go canoeing! / Nicole A. Mansfield.
Description: North Mankato, Minnesota : Capstone Press, [2023]
| Series: The wild outdoors | Includes bibliographical references. |
Audience: Ages 8–11 | Audience: Grades 4–6 | Summary: Get out
on the water and enjoy the sights and sounds of the great outdoors!
Readers will learn all about planning, paddling, and the gear they
need to take a canoe trip. They'll learn about safety and caring for
the environment while enjoying an outdoor canoeing adventure!—
Provided by publisher.
Identifiers: LCCN 2021057057 (print) | LCCN 2021057058 (ebook) |
ISBN 9781666345650 (hardcover) | ISBN 9781666345667 (paperback) |
ISBN 9781666345674 (pdf) | ISBN 9781666345698 (kindle edition)
Subjects: LCSH: Canoes and canoeing—Juvenile literature.
Classification: LCC GV784.3 .M36 2023 (print) | LCC GV784.3
(ebook) | DDC 797.122—dc23/eng/20211222
LC record available at https://lccn.loc.gov/2021057057
LC ebook record available at https://lccn.loc.gov/2021057058

Image Credits

Alamy: dpa picture alliance, 21; Getty Images: Ariel Skelley, Cover,
1, ImagineGolf, 7, Inti St Clair, 6, Larry Williams, 9, Per Breiehagen,
29; Shutterstock: Brocreative, 12, Shutterstock/damann, 27, Dan
Thornberg, 23, Elena Elisseeva, 18, GROGL, 11, Jeff Holcombe, 8,
Maridav, 17 (right), Phattaraphum, 17 (left), sianc, 5, Travis Modisette,
15, William Hager, 25, WiP-Studio, 13

Editorial Credits

Editor: Erika L. Shores; Designer: Dina Her; Media Researchers:
Jo Miller and Pam Mitsakos; Production Specialist: Tori Abraham

All internet sites appearing in back matter were available and accurate
when this book was sent to press.

Table of Contents

Words in **bold** are in the glossary.

Chapter 1

GET OUT ON THE WATER

Look! A shiny, silver fish just jumped out of the water. Listen! The calm water and gentle breeze are calling you. Birds are chirping and frogs are croaking. Where are you? You are out on the water in a canoe.

The first canoes were crafted thousands of years ago. The original purpose of the canoe was for water transportation. Canoes made daily tasks like hunting, fishing, and trading easier. Today, people mainly use canoes for fun and adventure on the water.

Canoeing is a popular outdoor activity. In 2019, almost 9 million Americans went canoeing. Canoeing is fun for people of all ages. It gets people outside and on the water. Canoers experience nature at its finest.

Paddling a canoe is a fun way to get around on a lake.

For many people, the best part of canoeing is gliding along in peaceful waters. Canoers enjoy getting away from busy neighborhoods or cities. Spending quality time with loved ones is another reason people go canoeing. Canoeing lets you enjoy nature up close. It doesn't harm animals, trails, or other natural environments.

Canoeing is good exercise. Paddling increases strength in your arms, legs, and **torso**. Taking deep breaths of fresh air is great for your lungs. It also helps lower stress levels. Spending time on the water and hearing its soothing sounds is calming. After paddling all day in your canoe, you can look back with pride at what you have accomplished.

People enjoy the calm, quiet waters during a canoe trip.

Spy It! Sketch It!

Your eyes will spy all kinds of treasures while canoeing. From birds and fish to clouds up above, there is a lot to see in nature. Take a sketch pad and pencil along on your trip. Scan your environment for special things to observe. Then, when you spy it, sketch it.

Chapter 2

CANOEING HOW-TOS

Planning the details of your canoe trip is important. You will need to decide where to canoe. You will need to check the weather forecast so you know what to wear.

Learning how to canoe safely is another part of preparing for your trip. You must wear a life jacket. In the canoe, avoid quick movements, as they can cause your canoe to flip over. Also, you should never canoe during bad weather.

Canoeing allows a group of people to spend time together outdoors.

Canoeing with friends or family is a way for people to connect. You paddle in sync and work as a team. Canoeing is safest and the most fun when you go with a partner or group. Children should never canoe alone.

People head to lakes to canoe, fish, and swim.

Canoe History

The word "canoe" as we use it today, began about 500 years ago. It comes from the South American Arawak Indian tribe's word "kanawa." The Arawaks used canoes to transport goods and to travel from island to island.

The water in lakes or ponds can be calm and gentle. Both are great places for a beginner to learn how to paddle. Rivers move fast and often have sharp turns. They are more difficult to paddle and turn in. Beginners should take their first outings on calm water with minimal **current.**

Joining a local canoe club lets you connect with people who know about canoeing where you live. You can look online for canoeing organizations. They are likely to have lists of paddling clubs in your area. Many clubs host events to bring canoers together throughout the year. Visiting local and state parks is another way to begin your research for good canoeing spots.

**Canoeing on a fast-moving river requires more skill
than canoeing on a calm lake.**

Knowing where to sit in the canoe is important to having a successful ride. The paddler with the most experience should sit in the back of the canoe. This is called the stern. The person in the stern is responsible for steering. It is best for the least-experienced canoer to sit in the front. It is called the bow. The person in the bow simply paddles.

bow

stern

To paddle, you will hold the grip and the shaft. The grip is the very top part of the paddle. The shaft is the long skinny center part. You'll dip the paddle into the water. Then, make sure that the blade is totally underneath the water. Finally, pull the blade backward through the water, pushing water out of your way. Repeating these steps moves your canoe through the water.

Parts of a Paddle

grip	the main handle
shaft	the long skinny part of the paddle, runs from the grip to the throat
throat	the bottom of the shaft, where the paddle starts to widen into the blade
shoulder	the widening section between the throat and the main blade
blade	the flat, wide bottom end that goes in the water
tip	the very bottom at the end of the blade

Depending on the climate where you live, most people canoe in spring, summer, and fall. Warm weather allows you to stop paddling and enjoy fishing, munching on snacks, or just watching the clouds roll by.

Always pay attention to the weather when canoeing. Never canoe in a thunderstorm. If you hear thunder before you start out, plan your trip for another day.

When you are out on the water, you are the tallest object in the area. That makes you a target for a lightning strike. Lightning always hits the highest object available. If you hear thunder or see lightning while canoeing, paddle to shore. Then you must wait for the storm to pass.

FACT

Never seek shelter under a tree during a thunderstorm. If you can't go inside a building, you should wait inside a vehicle during the storm.

Canoers must head for shore if the sky turns dark and stormy.

Chapter 3

SAFETY AND SUPPLIES

You'll need several supplies to ensure a great day on the water. A life jacket (also known as a personal flotation device or PFD) is essential gear. Always wear a PFD, and never take it off while you are out on the water.

Before leaving home, check the weather and water temperatures at the location where you will be canoeing. Apply plenty of sunscreen, even on a cloudy day. You can still get a sunburn when it's cloudy. Dress in layers of clothing. Make sure they are appropriate for the weather and water temperature.

Flip-flops or sandals are not the best choice for canoeing footwear. They can slip off your feet easily. Wear a water-safe swim shoe with a thick rubber sole. Rubber soles help prevent injuries from sharp rocks.

Use a personal flotation device (PFD) and wear water-safe shoes when you go canoeing.

Life Jacket Safety

- ☑ Check the label on the inside of your life jacket. It should list the height and weight range that is appropriate for that jacket's size.
- ☑ Check to be sure that the label states "Coast Guard Approved."
- ☑ Check the life jacket for holes and tears. Do not wear a ripped or torn jacket.
- ☑ Put on your life jacket and zip every zipper, buckle every buckle, and tighten every strap.

Canoeing is a great way to exercise, relax, and have fun. However, take the responsibility of staying alert while you are out on the water seriously. Sit in the middle of your seat at all times. Don't stand or kneel in a canoe without an adult's permission. Don't lean or jump over the side of your canoe without warning. You could tip the canoe and dump everyone and everything into the water.

Stay safe in a canoe by paying attention and following the rules.

All of that sun and paddling fun will drain your energy. Bring along plenty of water to drink. Pack a healthy snack, such as fruit or trail mix.

What to Bring with You

☑ life jacket
☑ layers of clothing
☑ water shoes
☑ sun hat
☑ sunscreen
☑ water
☑ healthy snacks
☑ trash container
☑ map of the area

Optional:
☑ lip balm
☑ clothes and towel
☑ fishing pole
☑ bait and tackle
☑ binoculars
☑ sketchbook and pencil

Canoeing in calm water, especially while wearing a life jacket, is usually safe. But there is always a chance your canoe could tip over. Know what to do in case you **capsize**.

If you find yourself under the water, stay calm and swim back up to the top. Your PFD will keep you afloat. Once your head is above water, grab your canoe and don't let go. If possible, turn the canoe upright with the help of your canoeing partner. Then, each of you should hold a side of the boat under one armpit. Then you both use your other arms to swim to shore with the canoe.

FACT

An average 16-foot (4.9-meter) canoe can hold about 940 pounds (426 kilograms).

If your canoe capsizes, a PFD will keep your head above water as you make your way to shore.

Chapter 4

TAKE CARE OF THE ENVIRONMENT

Many canoers enjoy fishing while out on the water. Learn your state and local fishing laws and regulations before you cast your line. Some fish are too small to eat or may even be **endangered**. In many states if you catch a fish of a certain type or size, you must release it back into the water.

Never throw trash or pour unwanted liquids overboard. Keep your trash contained. Be sure to bring along a simple solution for collecting your trash throughout the day. A small bucket with a lid or a simple plastic bag can be used to hold trash while canoeing. Back on dry land, empty your trash into the appropriate trash bin.

Fishing is a good way to enjoy the outdoors in a canoe.

It's important to drain, clean, and dry your canoe after every trip. You can do this by turning it upside down in a dry area. Clean and dry your paddles and any other gear too before heading home. Remove any mud, plants, or small creatures you might find. This will help keep organisms in the original body of water they were found in.

When organisms, such as snails, mussels, fish, or even plants are brought to a new body of water (for example by dirty canoe equipment) they are called **invasive species**. Invasive species are a problem because there is no **predator** to keep their growth under control.

Canoes, paddles, and other gear should be
clean and dry before you pack up to go home.

Invasive species may grow out of control. They can start to take over their new environment. Think about it. One weekend you canoe on a nearby lake. Muddy water gets trapped in the bottom of your canoe. Living inside that water are tiny organisms like snails or plants. You don't clean your canoe and the muddy water remains there.

The next weekend you travel several hours away to canoe on a different lake. When you put your canoe back in the water, there is a chance the tiny unseen snails, plants, and other organisms may still be alive. They might enter the new water and start to invade.

FACT

Zebra mussels are one of the most dangerous invasive species found in North America. These fingernail-size creatures attach themselves in huge clumps to any hard surface in the water.

Eurasian watermilfoil is an invasive plant that harms lakes.

Chapter 5

CANOE CAMPING

After you have made a few successful canoe trips, you might want to try canoe camping. This activity combines canoeing fun with camping adventure.

Canoe campers pack their backpacks with enough supplies to travel and camp for several days. Since gear will likely get wet, canoe campers pack everything in waterproof bags. They transport their backpacks, tents, and supplies in their canoe instead of on their backs while hiking. Canoeing lets campers travel to areas that are impossible to drive or hike to.

You've learned about canoeing basics, safety, and gear. Now, let's get paddling! Whether you canoe every weekend or once a year, adventure will meet you on the water every time.

Campers use canoes to reach remote areas away
from other people.

GLOSSARY

capsize (KAP-syz)—to tip over in the water

current (KUHR-uhnt)—the movement of water in a river or ocean

endangered (in-DAYN-juhrd)—at risk of dying out

invasive species (in-vay-SUHV SPEE-sheez)—a living thing that is put into a new place that it does not normally belong, eventually causing harm

predator (PRED-uh-tur)—an animal that hunts other animals for food

torso (TOR-soh)—the part of the body between the neck and the waist, not including the arms

READ MORE

Kingston, Seth. *Canoeing and Kayaking.* New York: PowerKids Press, 2022.

Paxton, John. *My Awesome Guide to Freshwater Fishing: Essential Techniques and Tools for Kids.* Emeryville, CA: Rockridge Press, 2021.

Simons, Lisa M. Bolt. *Go Freshwater Fishing!* North Mankato, MN: Capstone Press, 2022.

INTERNET SITES

10 Essential Canoeing Tips
vobs.org/blog/10-essential-canoeing-tips/

The Top 3 Basic Canoeing Strokes: Canoeing for Beginners
youtube.com/watch?v=cu4OaqlXOo0

The Ultimate Guide to Canoeing
canoeing.com/beginner/

INDEX

ABOUT THE AUTHOR

Nicole A. Mansfield is passionate about writing books for children. She loves to exercise and to sing at church. She lives with her husband and three children on a military base in Georgia.